**From the Minister of Food,
The Rt. Hon. LORD WOOLTON.**

" This is a Food War. Every extra row of vegetables in allotments saves shipping. If we grow more Potatoes we need not import so much Wheat. Carrots and Swedes, which can be stored through the winter, help to replace imported fruit.

" We must grow our own Onions. We can no longer import ninety per cent. of them, as we did before the war.

" The vegetable garden is also our National Medicine Chest—it yields a large proportion of the vitamins which protect us against infection.

" I therefore welcome this booklet which encourages people to grow more vegetables.

" The battle on the Kitchen Front cannot be won without help from the Kitchen Garden."

Halcon Picture Company

RATION BOOK RECIPES

Some Food Facts 1939-1954
Gill Corbishley

CONTENTS

ABOVE RIGHT: *Lord Woolton picks his lunch, 4th of December 1943.*
BELOW LEFT: *Introductory paragraph from 'The Vegetable Garden Displayed' 1941.*

Introduction

> "It was the habit of Mavis and her friends to have meals all day; they barely paused between breakfast, morning coffee, early lunch, afternoon coffee, afternoon tea, late tea, supper and bedtime snacks... It was the war that had done this to them, turning life into one continuous quest for food - food to take home, food to consume in shops, food no longer a means but life's great end. Rations, dictated by coupons, had to be bought; to leave them unbought would be a sinful waste; bacon, fats, sweets, biscuits, everything in tins, were week by week absorbed; people grew in stature and in weight, and clothes were let out."
> 'The World My Wilderness' Rose Macauley 1950

The six years of the Second World War were an extraordinary period for society at the time. These years also provided a watershed for many aspects of the social structure of Britain. Nowhere is this easier to discover than in people's diet.

Supply ships bringing in Britain's imports were blockaded by the German navy and at one time one out of every four was sunk. The impact of this was felt especially in naval towns like Portsmouth and Southampton. The blockade, combined with the overriding necessity to use shipping for troops, threw the country back upon its own resources for food supplies. Suddenly some of the staples of the British diet - meat, sugar and tea - were in drastically short supply. Imports of food between 1939 and 1945 were almost halved.

Before 1939 only one third of all the food eaten in Britain was actually grown in this country. By 1945 the number of acres under cultivation had risen to 18,000,000 from 12,000,000 in 1939 and two thirds of the nation's food was produced at home.

The impact on society was not confined to those few years. 'Austerity' and rationing dragged on until 1954. The habit of hoarding every stringy runner bean and giant marrow persists in many of today's 70-year-olds; nor can they restrain a look of horror if they should chance to see whole cartons of fried chicken thrown away in the gutter. The social history of the twentieth century would have been very different if it had not been split by that traumatic period.

This booklet provides a summary of the particular effects of the war on food and cooking which could be used to expand a study of Second World War monuments and materials or as part of a general look at the war years.

Official attitudes to diet and recipes from these years have been collected from original sources. There are suggestions for further reading and for school work on historic, technological and language projects.

ABOVE LEFT: Illustration from 'Food from Overseas' 1941.

Administration

The organisation of the civilian population during the war is in itself worthy of historical study. The government set up the Food (Defence Plans) Department as early as November 1936. The task of feeding the fighting forces so that they stayed strong and healthy almost pales into insignificance when compared with the enormous problem of feeding the back-up workers in factories, on the land and in offices (not to mention the population at large). On the 29th September 1939 the National Register was set up and everybody was supplied with an identity card. By January 1940 ration-books had been issued and butter, bacon and sugar were 'on the ration'. In March of that year meat was first rationed and in May a 'Limitation of Supplies Order' restricted the production of non-essential consumer goods.

Rationing seems to have worked well in most of the country through the war. Although there was a 'black market' in London and other towns, it does not seem to have been as damaging as the 'black market' in Germany and the occupied countries. Perhaps the main responsibility for this success should be attributed to the newly-created Ministry of Food and, especially, to the Minister, Lord Woolton.

Girls busy filling in ration books at the Food Executive Office in London.

DOCTOR CARROT *guards your Health*

'I'll put pep in your step.' says Potato Pete

The **KITCHEN FRONT**

122 WARTIME RECIPES

broadcast by Frederick Grisewood, Mabel Constanduros and others, specially selected by the Ministry of Food.

6D. NET

The Ministry employed cooks, such as Marguerite Patten, to staff their advice centres in places like school kitchens and the foyer at Harrods. The public was bombarded with help and guidance, via Food Facts in magazines, Food Flashes at the cinema and the daily five-minute radio programme Kitchen Front, which was on every morning after the eight o'clock news. Who could forget, or fail to respond to, jingles like:

"Those who have the will to win
Cook potatoes in their skin
Knowing that the sight of peelings
Deeply hurts Lord Woolton's feelings"?

Eighteen million people listened every day to Charles Hill 'The Radio Doctor', and learned which foods were good for them and how to cook them. 'Potato Pete' was only rivalled by 'Doctor Carrot' and one, or both, of them tended to turn up in almost every recipe.

The government's publicity efforts were not simply confined to helping the public to use the sorts of food easily available. In order for that extra 6,000,000 acres to produce food, campaigns such as DIG FOR VICTORY and drives to recruit land girls and to persuade not only "the big man with the plough" but "the little man with the spade" to turn every spare yard of earth over to the production of food were constantly underway. Those with suitable gardens were encouraged to keep chickens and a pig, and could discover how to cook every bit of them in booklets like Good Housekeeping's '100 Recipes for Unrationed Meat Dishes'.

G FOR VICTORY

Imperial War Museum

BELOW LEFT: From Good Housekeeping's '100 Recipes for Unrationed Meat Dishes'.

LAMB'S PLUCK

1 lamb's pluck
1 onion, sliced
1 carrot, diced
Sprig of thyme and parsley
1 bay leaf   Salt, pepper
Vinegar   Olive oil   Little mace
2 oz. butter or margarine
Flour   Stock

Wash the pluck and cut it up small. Put it into an earthenware basin with all the ingredients except the butter, flour and stock. Soak for 12 hours, turning frequently.

Melt the butter in a pan, add the minced pluck and stew for a little while. Dust with flour, cover with stock and stew till tender. Serve with the gravy strained over it.

5

These efforts were not unsuccessful. Allotments flourished in many a London park, like Hampstead Heath - fertile, convenient for large numbers of householders but unfortunately not numerous enough to counteract completely the deficiencies in everyone's diet. Green vegetables, fruit and eggs from home range hens were still not available for many people during the war years. A limiting factor for many would-be poultry farmers was the fact that grain for chicken food was as scarce as for bread-manufacture.

'Points' were introduced into food ration books on December 1st 1941. They had been necessary for clothes since June; now tinned foods, which had previously been unrationed, could only be bought if one had both enough money and enough points left from the sixteen allocated to each person every month, to afford them. Naturally, the scarcer and more nutritious (or more appetising) food cost more points.

TOP: *Hampstead Heath Allotments, 1941.*
LEFT: *Vegetables growing in the moat at the Tower of London, June 1940.*
RIGHT: *Fruit in tins is released, January 1943. The release of canned fruit and vegetables is the main feature on the food front.*

Adjustment

Violet Plimmer, author of 'Food Values in War Time' published in 1941, begins her book: "The joys of the rationing system can only be fully appreciated by those who had to cater for a family during the last war". She maintains that millions of hours were spent queuing for food during the 1914-18 War and that "the biggest pusher or the owner of the swankiest fur coat got served first". Her pious hope that rationing would eliminate queuing was not realised in the next few years. For many people the only way to get hold of the 'optional extras' such as offal or onions was to join a queue. Price regulation and ration-books did their best to ensure that much of the staple food which was available was distributed fairly but scarce supplies meant that the customer who wanted the best meat and the freshest vegetables was still forced to queue.

But how to find substitutes for the variety of ordinary foods like onions, eggs, cheese, bananas, tomatoes, sausages, meat, fish, cakes, biscuits, chocolate, apples, oranges and lemons? Valiant efforts were made. In 1942 the Ministry of Food published the advertisement 'Fruitful results from Vegetables', which suggested that the daily requirement of Vitamin C should be obtained by eating a 'good portion' of raw shredded sprouts, raw shredded spinach or shredded swede or turnip. "The Vitamin C value will be increased if you use parsley or mustard and cress as a garnish", the advertisement adds encouragingly. It was also suggested that mashed parsnips flavoured with banana essence would be difficult to distinguish from the genuine article!

Dried egg powder from America was available from 1942 and a tin containing the equivalent of a dozen eggs was offered for each consumer registered for shelleggs, "extra to your regular egg ration". Experiments were also made with dried vegetables, but on the whole these were so unpalatable that it took another twenty years before anyone tried to market dried vegetables commercially in England.

BELOW: Queue in Streatham High Street for still unrationed bread, 20th July 1946. Huge queues formed themselves outside bakers' shops all over London on the last day before the introduction of bread rationing.
BELOW RIGHT: Housewife purchasing the soap ration for two. Soap was rationed on the 9th of February 1942. Soap, soap flakes and soap powders for domestic use were rationed and could be bought only by surrendering coupons or permits.

The population were exhorted to save fuel, as well as making the most of the ingredients available, by cooking conservatively. Porridge cooked overnight in a haybox satisfied both these requirements and the ubiquitous Ministry of Food was quick to encourage such economies as an individual portable hay-box as a Christmas gift: "You can make the portable hay-box from a spare gas-mask carrier. It's very simple. Full directions will be sent if you write to the Ministry of Food". One big baking session per week and the use of a pressure-cooker were other fuel economies advocated.

Married women engaged in war work might be able to avoid the added burden of queuing for food. The government issued a priority shopping card which should have guaranteed its possessor immediate service. The demand for women workers to replace men who were in the armed forces also led to radical change in many a housewife's lifestyle. The touching advertisement which describes the quandary of the ARP Warden who couldn't give her husband a hot pudding until she discovered MRS PEEK's PUDDINGS illustrates an acceleration of change for both the average married woman and the food industry!

Mass catering - works canteens and, later, the Government-run British restaurants - helped to supplement many people's rations. In Sheffield the Civic Restaurants, controlled by the City Council, were so successful that, in a Daily Telegraph news item in 1947, Councillor J. Morris said that the Council intended to continue as restaurateurs: "It will be useless for private traders to squeal about it".

Let the Hay-box cook for you. Stews, soups, haricot beans, porridge or root vegetables will cook by themselves in a hay-box. Allow at least twice as long as for ordinary simmering. If necessary, food can be left to cook in the box all day or all night. The secret of success in hay-box cookery is to put the food into the box *boiling* hot and to "hot up" before serving.

"It was always a bad day when you had to go to the British Restaurant. Maybe the little cafe round the corner served nothing much better in the way of food: but you felt Mrs. Bolton's variations of the theme of spam and chips were by some indefinable advantage of individuality and privacy an improvement on the anonymous offerings of the British Restaurant. Eating in the British Restaurant was awfully like being fed by the Government - positively by the Minister of Food himself."
'A Cack-handed War' Edmund Blishen 1972

"Not mustard, Bobbums, though well you might have thought so, for what you do need with all this American tinned stuff, though it is wonderful of them to lease-lend us all their Spam and what not, is mustard."
'Growing Up' Angela Thirkell 1945

Health

One, almost incidental, by-product of the necessity for both organisation and adjustment of food supplies and diet throughout the country between 1939 and 1945, was actually an overall improvement in the health of the British people. In 1939 half the people of Britain were suffering from some degree of malnutrition. Although the average daily consumption of calories was 3000 in both 1939 and 1945 great changes in distribution had been achieved. Lord Woolton's National Milk Scheme concentrated limited supplies on 'priority' adults and on children and by 1943 consumption of milk per head had tripled in some areas. The Government's Vitamin Welfare Scheme for children, which was introduced in December 1941, supplied children with cod liver oil and later with orange juice. The absence of imported grain coupled with the Government's determination to impose health on the population and to avoid bread rationing (which it did - until after the war) led to the introduction of the National Loaf in 1941. This was made of home-grown flour which contained not less than 85% of the whole grain, was grey in colour and was extremely unpopular with most of the people of Britain.

In 1934 the School Medical Officer for Glossop designed a free school meal to supply school-children suffering from malnutrition with the constituents missing from their home food. The war-time Glossop Health Sandwich consisted of:

> 1 pint of milk and 1 orange, when obtainable;
> if no fruit $\frac{1}{4}$ oz chopped parsley is included in the Sandwich filling.
> 3 oz of wholemeal bread
> $\frac{3}{4}$ oz butter or vitaminized margarine
> $\frac{3}{4}$ oz salad; mustard and cress, or watercress, or lettuce or tomato or carrot
> 1 $\frac{1}{2}$ oz cheese, or salmon, or herring, or sardine or liver
> $\frac{3}{16}$ oz dried brewers' yeast.

The affluent minority of the population in 1939 also actually benefited from the wartime regime. In 'It's That Meal Again', a BBC TV programme shown on 31st December, 1989, adults spending six weeks on a war-time diet showed a small reduction in weight and a significant drop in the level of cholesterol in their blood. As Violet Plimmer points out: "Highly seasoned foods and drinks, sweet or stimulating, iced or unnaturally hot, give an immediate and fictitious sense of well-being and are very popular. Many of these delights have vanished or are restricted in amount and will become ever more rare as the war goes on. Luckily they are unnecessary and their absence may toughen rather than weaken our fibre and powers of resistance. In spite of many inconveniences, we have (at the time of writing, January 1941) suffered no limitations that will undermine health if the foods that are available are suitably combined". Back to Clara Carrot and Potato Pete! But it's worth remembering that national malnutrition during the First World War had peaked when the potato crop failed in 1917 and that thousands died in the subsequent influenza epidemic.

"*I must say I rather like this beige bread.*"

Walt Disney
Clara Carrot

"Dear me," said Robert, having received his (bread), "Mrs. Rodney and I forgot about bringing our own butter." This served to draw Stella's attention to the butter arrangements: each one of the family had his or her own ration placed before his or her own plate in a differently coloured china shell.'
'The Heat of the Day' Elizabeth Bowen 1949

BELOW RIGHT: From 'The Life of an Airman's Wife'.

Hulton Picture Company

The Battlefront

One section of the community was exempt from the constant need to be inventive with food.

"The food for the Army is planned to imitate the diet that was most popular in peace-time for those who could afford it. Food-stuffs of animal origin appear, if possible, at three meals a day", writes Violet Plimmer. The War Office issued a "Manual of Military Cooking and Dietary" in 1940 which amply illustrates this point: meat, tea, eggs and sugar figure as essential ingredients in soldiers' menus. "Thousands of women aged 17½ - 50 wanted to become cooks in the ATS and WAAF" ran the advertisements and many a hapless girl soon found herself back at school labor-iously keeping her 'Progress of Work Log Book' and copying down recipes such as

Sea Pie Per Hundred Men

25lbs meat (unprepared), 50lbs potatoes (prepared), 4 ozs pars-ley, 6lbs onions, 16lbs flour, 6lbs suet, 4 ozs baking powder, 4 ozs salt, water to bind.

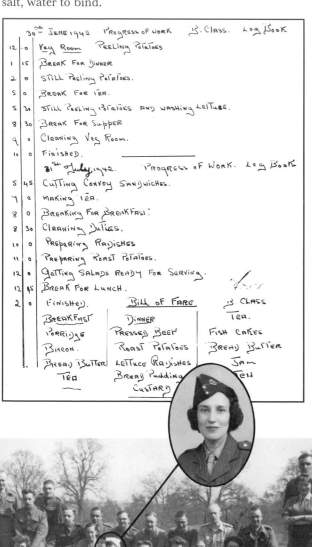

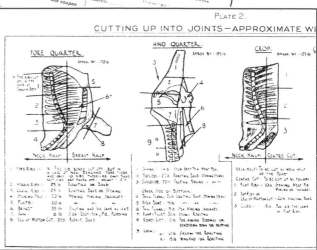

ABOVE: Cutting up joints, from the 'Manual of Military Cooking and Dietary' 1940.

LEFT & BELOW: From Psyche Corbishley's 'Progress of Work Book'.
BELOW LEFT: ATS unit in Norfolk 1942:
INSET: Psyche Corbishley.

When the army was on the move at the front, ingenious devices such as the Bluff portable stove and the Aldershot Oven were used and army catering chiefs fought with ounces of food and milligrammes of vitamins to create the one-day individual landing-rush ration in its waterproof box 6″x5″x2″ (15cm x 13 cm x 5cm) in volume. The box contained dehydrated meat, biscuit, solid sweetened oatmeal, chocolate, tea-cubes, soup-cubes, boiled sweets and chewing-gum and supplied approximately 4,000 calories. Vitamin tablets were also supplied to supplement the soldier's diet, as the Government were very aware of the need to avoid diseases such as pellagra, beriberi and scurvy, which had been common among soldiers in all previous wars.

Below and overleaf are some menus for comparison. Compare the week's menus for the army, as dictated to an ATS recruit in 1942, with the menu for civilians quoted from 'War at Home' by Fiona Reynoldson and B. Seebohm Rowntree's menu for a labourer in York in 1901. The monotony and vitamin deficiencies in many people's diet in pre-war Britain are easily observed.

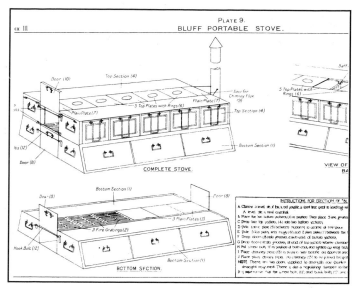

ABOVE: From 'Manual of Military Cooking and Dietary' 1940.

Breakfast

	1901	1942 Home Front	1942 Battle Front	
Monday	Bread bacon butter tea	Porridge black treacle no milk	Prunes egg and fried bread bread and butter tea with milk	
Tuesday	Bread bacon butter coffee	Porridge as usual	Porridge milk fish bread and butter tea	
Wednesday	Bread bacon butter tea	Porridge as usual	Porridge milk toad in the hole bread and butter tea	
Thursday	Bread butter coffee	Porridge as usual	Porridge milk bacon bread and butter tea	
Friday	Bread butter tea	Porridge as usual	Porridge milk sausages bread and butter jam tea	
Saturday	Bread bacon coffee	One slice of bacon and a piece of fried bread	Porridge milk boiled egg bread and butter jam tea	
Sunday	Bread butter shortcake coffee	One slice of bacon fried egg fried bread	Porridge milk egg and bacon fried bread bread and butter tea	

Dinner

	1901	1942 Home Front	1942 Battle Front	
Monday	Pork potatoes pudding tea	Jam sandwiches	Cottage pie mashed potatoes cauliflower damson pie	
Tuesday	Pork bread tea	Potato crisp sandwiches	Meat and potato pie cabbage doughnuts custard	
Wednesday	Bacon and eggs potatoes bread tea	Cheese sandwiches	Preserved meat fritters chips cabbage baked rice pudding	
Thursday	Bread bacon tea	Potato crisp sandwiches	Cream of lettuce soup brown stew mashed potatoes green peas pancakes	
Friday	Bread butter toast tea	Spam sandwiches	Potato soup braised beef braised rice fondant potatoes stewed prunes	
Saturday	Bacon potatoes pudding tea	Bread and cheese	Meat pie buttered cabbage savoury potatoes pineapple chunks	
Sunday	Pork onions potatoes Yorkshire pudding	One lamb chop carrots potatoes blackberry and apple pie	Roast beef Yorkshire pudding roast potatoes pear flan	

Tea

	1901	1942 Home Front	1942 Battle Front	
Monday	Bread butter tea	Corned beef stew with soya bean dumpling bread & peanut butter	Fish cakes bread and butter jam tea	
Tuesday	Bread butter boiled eggs tea	Whalemeat carrots potatoes suet pudding	Boiled ham bread and butter jam tea	
Wednesday	Bread butter tea	Scrambled dried eggs stewed apples	Welsh Rarebit bread and butter jam tea	
Thursday	Bread butter tea	Baked potatoes cake made with dried eggs	Lettuce and pies bread and butter jam tea	
Friday	Bread butter tea	Liver one sausage potato bread and butter	Fish bread and butter jam tea	
Saturday	Bread butter shortcake tea	Dried egg omelette cabbage potatoes carrot flan	Pasties bread and butter tea	
Sunday	Bread butter shortcake tea	Potato pie bread and butter jam	Sausage rolls lettuce bread and butter jam tea	

How millions Sleep their way to health with Ovaltine

Cocoa, more bread and butter, or tea and a kipper or the odd slice of meat might by added as supper to the 1901 diet, while the army were served cocoa and a 'buffet' before they went to bed. On the Home Front, the meagre milk supply made cocoa and much-advertised Ovaltine a luxury which could only be approximated with reconstructed National Dried Milk!

"Now, you have had fresh tea made for me, Lady Waring, and you shouldn't," said Matron. "What would our good Lord Woolton say? But I shall throw patriotism to the winds and have a refreshing cup if you will let me."
'Growing Up' Angela Thirkell 1945.

Recipes

"Mrs George Pollett, wife of the Sheep's Head, was renowned far and wide for her fried fish and her steak and kidney puddings, which, alas, were now but beautiful memories. Yet even under the peculiar arrangements for fish known as zoning, a word accepted placidly by the population of England and with their genius for misinterpretation at once reduced to a synonym of total disappearance, Mrs. Pollett managed to do wonders with an occasional bit of frozen cod, and her meat ration always went twice as far as anyone else's".
'Growing Up' Angela Thirkell 1945

FOOD FROM OVERSEAS
RECIPES
FOOD EDUCATION MEMO. No. 4
ISSUED BY THE BOARD OF EDUCATION
PUBLISHED BY H.M. STATIONERY OFFICE
PRICE THREEPENCE

PRESERVES FROM THE GARDEN
"GROWMORE" BULLETIN No. 3
OF THE MINISTRY OF AGRICULTURE
AND FISHERIES PUBLISHED BY
HIS MAJESTY'S STATIONERY OFFICE
PRICE 4d. NET

Good Eating
SUGGESTIONS FOR WARTIME DISHES
2/-
a new selection of
Daily Telegraph
READERS' TESTED RECIPES
HUTCHINSON

The ABC of Cookery
PRICE · ONE SHILLING

100 RECIPES FOR UNRATIONED MEAT DISHES 6D

These recipes are taken from contemporary cookery books or from government-issued leaflets and advertisements. They are acknowledged by the following codes:

GE   'Good Eating: suggestions for Wartime Dishes'
WCB 'Wartime Cookery Book'
GR   Government Recipes
GF   'Good Fare'

Mock Hare Soup

—— 3 to 4 persons ——

2 large potatoes	2 cloves
1 leek	1 ½ pints stock or water
1 carrot	½ oz dripping
1 stick celery	Pepper and salt to taste
½ turnip	1 teaspoonful meat essence
5 ozs coarse oatmeal	or cube

Chop vegetables, put in pan with dripping and fry thoroughly. Add oatmeal and cook until brown, stirring all the time to prevent burning. Add seasoning, cloves, and stock and cook ½ hour on low heat. Sieve before serving, add meat essence and re-heat. (GE)

Sardine Fritters

—— 4 to 5 persons ——

1 tin sardines and batter ingredients as follows:

3 tablespoonfuls flour	1 egg
milk	salt and pepper

Method - Leave the sardines to drain from the oil. Put the flour in a basin with the salt and pepper. Put the yolk of the egg in a well in the centre and add enough milk to form a smooth batter. Beat up the white of egg and stir in lightly. Place a sardine on a tablespoon and dip the spoon in the batter to coat the fish. Dry fry in a lightly greased frying-pan, turning the fritters once. Drain on paper and decorate with parsley and slices of lemon. (WCB)

Poor Man's Goose

—— 4 to 5 persons ——

¾ lb potatoes	½ lb liver or pig's fry
2 oz gravy beef (optional)	2 small onions
½ teaspoonful dried sage	cold water
1 oz flour	salt and pepper

Method - Mix the flour and seasoning together. Cut the meat into even-sized pieces and roll them in the seasoned flour. Place in a pie-dish with layers of sliced onion and sage. Peel the potatoes and half-cook them. Cut them in thick slices and place over the top of the meat. Three-parts fill the dish with water, cover with greased paper and bake in a moderate oven (350°F) for about 1 hour. (WCB)

Vitality Mould

—— 4 to 5 persons ——

3 lb spinach	pepper and salt
2 beaten eggs	a little allspice
pinch of mixed herbs	7 tablespoonfuls fine white
1 oz margarine	breadcrumbs

Method - Wash the spinach thoroughly in several changes of water. Put into a large saucepan with a very little salt and cook slowly without the addition of any extra water until it is quite tender. Rub through a sieve. Melt the margarine in a saucepan. Stir in the sieved spinach. Season. Add the herbs, breadcrumbs, and beaten egg. Blend well and put into a well-greased basin. Cover with greased paper and steam until the mixture is set and firm, about 30-45 minutes. Serve with white sauce. (WCB)

Beetroot and Celery

—— 4 to 5 persons ——

2 or 3 cooked beetroots,	salt and pepper
depending on size	lemon juice
5 or 6 stalks celery	a little margarine or dripping
a little chopped parsley	

Method - Cook the celery in boiling salted water, drain well. Chop into conveniently-sized pieces. Cut the beetroot into similarly-sized pieces and place in a pan together with the celery. Add the margarine or dripping, lemon juice, chopped parsley, and seasoning and stir together over a gentle heat until thoroughly hot. (WCB)

Eggless Salad Dressing

3 tablespoonfuls evaporated	a little made mustard
milk	2 tablespoonfuls olive oil
1 dessertspoonful vinegar	1 teaspoonful lemon juice
½ level teaspoonful salt	pepper

Method - Whip the evaporated milk until frothy. Add the oil very slowly, beating hard all the time. Continue to beat until the sauce thickens. Add the seasonings, lemon juice and vinegar, and blend thoroughly. (WCB)

Peanut Salad

1 tablespoonful peanut
   butter
2 tablespoonfuls mashed
   potato
1 teaspoonful chopped
   onion or 2 teaspoonfuls
   chives

Sliced beetroot or tomato
Lettuce
Salad dressing
A little grated cheese or
   chopped ham
Seasoning

Put peanut butter, potato, onion and seasoning in bowl. Beat well together, form into small balls. Mount each on slice of beetroot or tomato.

Arrange lettuce leaves in bowl and place mounted peanut balls on them. Serve salad dressing separately and a dish of grated cheese or of thinly sliced chopped ham. (GE)

Portman Pudding

—— 3 to 4 persons ——

6 ozs flour, 4 ozs each grated raw carrot and potato. Teaspoon mixed spice, 2 tablespoons sugar. Level teaspoon bicarbonate of soda, pinch of salt. ½ cupful of sultanas and raisins, 2 ozs fat. Cream fat and sugar, add carrot, potato, flour, spice and soda. Mix well together. Add fruit. Add water if necessary to make a stiff dropping consistency. Steam for 2 hours at least. A sweet that needs little sugar! (GR)

Raspberry Snow

—— 4 to 5 persons ——

2 oz sago
¼ pint water
2 tablespoonfuls raspberry
   jam

1 pint milk
2 oz sugar
a little lemon juice

Method - Boil the milk and water, sprinkle in the washed sago and cook thoroughly. Add the sugar. Allow to cool and beat up with the raspberry jam and the lemon juice. Add a little red colouring matter if liked. Serve alone or with fruit. (WCB)

FOOD IS A MUNITION OF WAR

Baked or Boiled Custard

3 reconstituted eggs
1 pint household milk
1 tablespoonful sugar

Few drops vanilla essence
Grate of nutmeg
Small piece of margarine

Stir sugar into eggs, add warm milk and vanilla. Pour in fireproof dish, adding margarine flaked in tiny pieces and nutmeg on top. Stand dish in oven in tin of hot water or on asbestos mat to prevent curdling. Stir custard before it sets so that margarine is well mixed with other ingredients. (GE)

Mock Clotted Cream

—— Dried Milk Method ——

1 tablespoonful dried
   milk
2 ozs margarine

1 teaspoonful sugar
Few drops of vanilla essence

Beat margarine and sugar together. By degrees add dried milk. Flavour with vanilla and beat until very smooth. (GE)

A clear plate
means
A clear conscience

Don't take more than you can eat

Wine

"I say, I hope there'll be something to drink tonight. The wine outlook becomes increasingly desperate since France went. One didn't expect to have to fight a war on an occasional half-pint of bitter, and lucky if you find that."
'The Soldier's Art' Anthony Powell 1966

To Preserve Beans in Salt

To every 3 or 4 lbs. beans allow 1 lb. salt. Beans must be young, fresh and tender. Do not wash unless necessary. If washed, dry before slicing. Cut them up, if small they may be left whole. Place a good layer of salt in a stoneware jar and on the salt a layer of beans. Continue to fill up jar with alternate layers, pressing beans well down and having top layer of salt. Cover and leave a few days. The beans shrink and the jar may then be filled up with more beans and salt, but take care that the final layer of salt completely covers the beans. Cover jar securely with lid or several layers of paper; if with cork paint over with melted paraffin wax. If the jar is stored in a room with a stone floor, place on a piece of wood.

To use beans: Remove from salt and soak in 2 or 3 lots of cold water for 12 hours at least. Cook in boiling water till tender. (GF)

'Lord Woolton Pie'

—— 5 to 6 persons ——

'Take 1 lb each of diced potatoes, cauliflower, swedes and carrots, three or four spring onions, if possible one teaspoonful of vegetable extract and one tablespoonful of oatmeal. Cook all together for 10 mins, with just enough water to cover. Stir occasionally to prevent the mixture from sticking. Allow to cool; put into a pie dish, sprinkle with chopped parsley, and cover with a crust of potatoes or wholemeal pastry. Bake in a moderate oven until the pastry is nicely brown and serve hot with a brown gravy. (GR)

Vegetable and Oatmeal Goulash

—— 3 to 4 persons ——

1 lb mixed root vegetables	1 teaspoonful meat essence
2 ozs coarse or medium	or cube
oatmeal	Sprinkling of paprika
Knob of dripping	Chopped parsley and herbs
Vegetable stock	to flavour
Pepper and salt to taste	

Prepare and dice vegetables. Fry in dripping until slightly cooked; add oatmeal and stir over fire until fat is absorbed. Season with herbs, pepper and salt and add meat extract. Cover with vegetable stock and simmer gently for 1 hour.

A little corned beef, cooked meat or fish may be added last thing. (GE)

Boston Bake

—— 4 to 5 persons ——

Soak 2 breakfastcupfuls small white beans in cold water for 24 hours. Put into a stew-jar with 3 ozs of diced fat bacon, and 1 lb sliced carrots. Mix thoroughly 1 level teaspoonful dry mustard and 1 tablespoonful golden syrup with enough hot water to make ½ pint. Pour over beans, and add enough water to cover. Put on lid, and bake in moderate oven for 2 to 2½ hours. For the last half-hour remove the lid and bring some of the bits of bacon to the top to brown off. Delicious! (GR)

Curried Carrots

—— 4 persons ——

Carrots	1 oz margarine or dripping
1½ teaspoonfuls curry	1 onion
powder	½ pint stock or water
3 teaspoonfuls flour	Pepper and salt

Trim carrots and boil in the usual way. Prepare curry sauce as follows. Melt fat in saucepan, add onion chopped, and fry a few minutes. Add curry powder and flour and fry, stirring from time to time, for a few minutes longer. Stir in stock or water, and when boiling, season to taste. Simmer gently about 30 minutes.

Add cooked carrots to curry sauce in saucepan and cook 20-30 minutes. Serve with a garnish of cooked rice (GF)

Baked Cod with Parsnip Balls and Piquant Sauce

—— 4 persons ——

2 lb parsnips,
salt, pepper,
browned crumbs,
1 lb soaked salt cod,
4 tablespoons dripping.

Sauce: ½ oz margarine,
2 level tablespoons flour,
½ pint vegetable stock,
salt, pepper, mustard,
1 tablespoon vinegar.

Cook the parsnips till quite soft. Drain and mash well with seasonings. Form into balls and coat in browned crumbs. Skin and bone fish, place in baking tin and spread with dripping. Bake in a quick oven for 5 minutes, then add parsnip balls and bake together for 20 minutes.

Sauce: Melt margarine, add flour, cook 3 minutes. Add liquid gradually, stirring well, and cook for another 5 minutes. Season and stir in vinegar. Serve with fish in centre of dish, the parsnip balls round and the sauce over the fish. (GR)

Passion Dock Pudding

Boil tender dock leaves with green onions or spring onions (or if not available then with ordinary onions). When cooked add a handful of oatmeal or wheatmeal, one beaten-up egg and a teaspoonful of butter or margarine. Simmer for half an hour.

The nutritive value of this Square Meal recipe would be increased by the inclusion of some yeast extract. (GR)

Egg and Rice Loaf

—— 3 persons ——

1 pint vegetable boilings
3 oz rice
3 dried eggs (reconstituted)
1 tablespoonful chopped
    parsley
Parsley or tomato sauce to
    serve

1 tablespoonful chopped
    onion
1 tablespoonful tomato
    sauce
Seasonings

Put the rice into a saucepan with the stock, cover and cook gently until the rice is tender and all the stock absorbed. Reconstitute the eggs and add them to the rice with the parsley, onion, tomato sauce and seasonings. Turn into a greased pudding basin or a cake tin and steam or bake in a moderate oven (375°F) until the mixture is set. This will take about 1 hour. Turn out and serve with parsley or tomato sauce. (GR)

Norfolk Pudding

—— 4 to 5 persons ——

1 pint milk
1 oz currants
1 oz candied peel
1 ½ oz sugar
pinch of salt

3 oz rice
2 oz sultanas
2 oz suet
a little grated nutmeg

Method - Wash the rice well and cook in the milk, using a double saucepan if one is available. Chop the suet and peel finely, add to the rice with peel, currants and sultanas. Add the sugar, nutmeg and salt, and beat all together thoroughly. Put into a well-greased pie-dish and bake in a slow oven for a few minutes. (WCB)

Cake or Pudding

¾ lb hot mashed potatoes
4 to 6 ozs dripping, lard
    or suet or mixture
2 ozs sugar

3 ozs sultanas or other dried
    fruit
Pinch of salt
Flour to bind
Nutmeg

Mix a little flour with potatoes to bind, work in fat, add sultanas, sugar, salt and nutmeg. Add more flour to make fairly stiff dough.

Put in greased shallow tin, bake in slow oven till crisp and brown. Serve hot for tea or with custard as luncheon sweet. (GE)

Apricot Upside Down Pudding

—— 4 to 5 persons ——

8 oz flour	3 oz suet
1 heaped teaspoonful baking-powder	pinch salt
	2 oz dried apricots
little milk for mixing	½ teaspoonful cinnamon
	3 oz sugar

Method - Soak the apricots overnight if possible. Chop the suet finely and mix with the flour, salt, baking-powder, sugar and cinnamon. Grease a cake tin, and decorate the bottom with apricots. Chop the remaining fruit and add to the flour, etc. Mix with milk. Place in the cake tin, cover with greased paper, and steam for 2 hours. Serve with custard. (WCB)

Ginger Cream

—— 4 to 5 persons ——

1 packet orange jelly	2 oz preserved or crystallised ginger
water	
1 small tin evaporated milk	

Method - Dissolve the jelly in sufficient water and a little ginger syrup to make up to ¾ pint. Add the evaporated milk and the preserved or crystallised ginger chopped into small pieces when almost set. Stir slightly in order to distribute the ginger evenly. Turn into a wetted mould. Stand in a cool place to set. (WCB)

Crunchies

5 ozs plain flour	4 ozs margarine, lard or clarified dripping
4 ozs medium oatmeal	
2 ozs sugar	2 ozs syrup
1 teaspoonful baking powder	Vanilla flavouring

Cream together the fat, sugar and syrup. Add flour, oatmeal, baking powder and a few drops of vanilla. Knead until the mixture binds. Roll out about ¼ inch thick, cut into rounds or fingers. Bake in moderate oven till golden brown for about 20 minutes. These biscuits keep well stored in air-tight tins. (GE)

Pink Layer Party Cake

1 cupful self-raising flour	¼ cupful sugar
1 cupful pink blancmange or pudding powder	2 oz margarine
	2 dried eggs reconstituted in milk

Beat sugar and margarine together. Mix flour and blancmange powder together. Add egg and flour alternately to mixture. Beat well; bake in 2 greased sandwich tins for 20 minutes.

When cold spread with layer of jam. To ice, boil together 2 tablespoonfuls each sugar and water and small piece of margarine. Allow to cool, beat in sufficient pink blancmange powder to make icing of right colour and consistency. (GE)

Mock Marzipan

½ lb haricot beans	1 teaspoon almond essence
4 tablespoons sugar	1 tablespoon margarine
2 tablespoons ground rice	

Soak the beans for 24 hours, then cook until tender in fresh, unsalted water. Put them on a tin in a warm oven to get dry and floury. Rub them through a sieve. Beat the sugar into the bean puree, add the ground rice, warmed margarine and, finally, the flavouring. Beat until smooth. Any flavouring or colouring matter may be added. (GR)

"The main street was by now empty: today nothing more would happen. Before noon the housewives had swarmed, so completely, whitely, stripping the shops that one might ask oneself why these remained open. A scale or two adhered to the fishmonger's marble slab; the pastrycook's glass shelves showed a range of interesting crumbs; the fruiterer filled a longstanding void with fans of cardboard bananas and a 'Dig for Victory' placard; the greengrocer's crates had been emptied of all but earth by those who had somehow failed to dig hard enough. The butcher flaunted unknown joints of purplish meat in the confidence that these could not be bought; the dairy restricted itself to a china cow; the grocer, with costless courage, kept intact his stocks of dummy cartons and tins. In the confectioner's windows the ribbons bleached on dummy boxes of chocolate among flyblown cut-outs of pre-war blonds. Newsagents without newspapers gave out in angry red chalk that they had no matches either. Pasted inside a telephone booth, a notice asked one to telephone less."
'The Heat of the Day' Elizabeth Bowen 1949

Topic Suggestions For Use By Teachers

Here are some suggestions for class work. You will find that all satisfy at least one of the Attainment Targets in published National Curriculum subjects. For example:

Science Attainment Target 1 Level 9: Plan a range of exploratory techniques, for example, experiments, literature searches, data logging and analysis. (See Advertising B).

Mathematics Attainment Target 12 Level 2: Choose criteria to sort and classify objects; record results of observations or outcomes of events. (See Analysing the Evidence C).

Technology in the Programme of Study for Key Stage 3 levels 3-7; in satisfying needs and addressing opportunities, pupils should be taught to 'consider the influence of advertising on consumers.' (see Advertising C).

History Attainment Target 3 Level 2: 'recognise that historical sources can stimulate and help answer questions about the past.' (see Analysing the Evidence D).

English Attainment Target 3 Level 3: 'produce a range of types of non-chronological writing, for example, notes for an activity in science or design.' (see Cooking and Energy Saving C).

Pattern of Meals to Follow the Rules for Healthy Eating

Here is a suggestion for planning your meals to include all these body-building materials and vitamins every day. The dinner and supper meals can be reversed to suit individual households. For young children, tea should be the evening meal and supper, if any, would consist of a milky drink.

BREAKFAST MENU
PORRIDGE
(or other cereal or fruit with milk)
COOKED DISH
(Egg or bacon or fish, etc., with fried potatoes or fried bread)
NATIONAL or WHOLEMEAL BREAD
with
BUTTER or MARGARINE
and
MARMALADE or JAM
TEA or COFFEE
COCOA or MILK for children

MID-MORNING SNACK
Milk for children. Mid-meal snack for men or women doing heavy work. This should contain some building and vitamin foods, for example, cheese and salad sandwiches.

DINNER MENU
SOUP
(if desired)
MEAT
(or cheese or fish or egg)
FRESH VEGETABLES
(a green one several times weekly)
POTATOES
PUDDING
(Baked or steamed or cold pudding or fruit in season—with milk or custard)
In planning dinner, choose the animal food or "muscle builder" first, then choose a vegetable to go with it and potatoes. The pudding and soup are chosen to "fill up."
Note.—Dried peas, beans, lentils or oatmeal should be added to the meat, fish, cheese and egg dishes if the quantity of animal food is small through rationing or shortage.

TEA MENU
NATIONAL or WHOLEMEAL BREAD
with
BUTTER or MARGARINE
SPREAD or SANDWICH FILLING
(of shredded raw vegetables or yeast extract)
CAKES or BISCUITS or SCONES
JAM (if desired)
TEA
MILK for children

SUPPER or LUNCH MENU
MAIN DISH
(of cheese or fish or egg or other muscle builders)
VEGETABLE
or
RAW SALAD
POTATOES
BREAD
with
BUTTER or MARGARINE
JAM or HONEY or SYRUP
TEA or COFFEE
MILK or COCOA for children

From 'The ABC of Cookery' 1945.

Food and Nutrition

A. Photocopy pages 15-17 which chart comparative diets and ask pupils to record their own meals for one week in the blank column for comparison. Which diet would they prefer? Which do they think is healthiest?

OR complete the chart with a week's school lunches.

B. Obtain a list of the number of calories in common foods (the sort of list used by slimmers). Measure the number of calories in a day's meals of your choice and compare with the Model Diet outline in this extract from 'Food Values in Wartime'.

——— A Typical Day's Food for an Adult ———

"Having considered the quality and quantity of the individual components it is now possible to review the diet as a whole. Pandering more or less to popular taste and habit, I gave in my book, Food Values at a Glance, a model diet unit for 1 Man Value. The food quantities required for a household or establishment of any specified Man Value can be obtained by multiplying the unit the required number of times, making use of the energy coefficients for different ages.

To allow for waste the diet was calculated on a generous scale as regards energy value and animal protein and is at present beyond our rationed scope, but may be taken as a model when we begin feeding up after the war.

Model Diet Unit = 1 Man Value for 1 Day

	Calories
½ pint milk	190
1 egg or 4 oz cod flesh	85
4 oz lean meat	170
1 herring or 2 oz cheese	240
4 oz fat (meat fat, suet, butter, margarine)	920
18 oz wholemeal bread, flour, cake, pudding, etc	1,230
2 oz sugar (including jam, marmalade, syrup)	230
12 oz potatoes	288
1 orange or 2 apples and 1 banana	35
Salad	10
4 oz cooked greens	22
Total	3,420

This Diet Unit provided 54 g animal protein a day and fat and carbohydrate in suitable proportions. Vitamin A, 7,500 I.U.; vitamin C, 110 mg. ascorbic acid; vitamin B1, 890 I.U. (I.U. = International Units of Vitamins).

It is not possible to calculate out a revised version suitable to war conditions owing to the fluctuating state of food supplies from week to week and from one district to another. Working on this model and using the suggestions given for substitute-finding the housekeeper has to do the best she can. The total fuel and animal protein can be reduced to $\frac{7}{8}$ of the total or even to ¾. It may be possible to have the milk and an egg perhaps once or twice a week. The meat portion for one day will have to be spread over several days and the amount of cheese reduced from a hunk to a little grated cheese sprinkled over a thick soup or vegetables. Of bread too we should try to eat less, as wheat is mostly imported, and substitute for it oatmeal, which is home produced and contains more protein and fat than wheatmeal. Biscuits and cakes are becoming once-a-week luxuries. More potatoes and vegetables and any fruits raised in kitchen garden or allotments must be eaten to make up for the foods which have to be curtailed. When imported fruits are rare as much use as possible should be made of the wild berries, hips and haws and rowans which have a high value for vitamin A as well as for C. There are many other wild foods which can be used and those who have old herbals will find them a profitable study. To replace meat as much fish as can be afforded should be eaten especially of the fatty fishes like sprats, pilchards, herrings and mackerel which have the highest food value for the lowest prices. Dried peas and beans can be used in a variety of ways in soups and vegetable stews, in pies and rissoles and savoury pastes to replace meat and cheese. As already said, the curtailment of sugar may be grievous to many but will do them more good than harm."

Health

Vitamin deficiencies were very much feared by the authorities during the war. Advertisements illustrated in the booklet stress the need for Vitamins A, C, & D and explain which foods supply them.

"The ordinary pre-war diet was not wholesome. It contains too many unwholesome foods, such as white bread, sugar, fats of low vitamin value, vegetables overcooked or wrongly cooked. To restore its wholesomeness such a diet required many additions." 'Food Values in Wartime'. 1941

A. Find and list the special foods and vitamins supplied to children during rationing.

The Vitamins

There are four vitamins especially which must be included regularly in the diet for health. These are Vitamin A, Vitamin B, Vitamin C and Vitamin D.

Vitamin A is needed for growth, for keeping the linings of the breathing, digestive and reproductive systems in good condition, and for the health of the eyes. It is found in cod liver oil, oily fish such as pilchards, herrings or salmon, dairy foods, and green and yellow vegetables. Liver, which is the animal's chief storehouse for important food material, is also rich in Vitamin A.

Vitamin B is needed for good digestion and steady nerves. It is got from National bread or flour, oatmeal, potatoes, peas, beans and lentils, yeast, eggs; vegetables also give a certain amount.

Vitamin C is needed for buoyant health, good skin, vitality and endurance. It comes chiefly from green vegetables, citrus fruit and potatoes. Orange juice concentrate, black-currant and rose-hip syrup are all very rich in Vitamin C. Babies should have these until they can take large quantities of vegetables.

Vitamin D is needed by children especially as it "anchors" the calcium in the proper places in growing bones and teeth and makes them strong. It comes from cod liver oil, butter and margarine, and fat fish such as pilchards, herrings, salmon, etc. Sunshine on a child's skin also helps to give this vitamin, but in this climate there is not very much sunshine, and so it is important that children, especially young ones, should have cod liver oil every day.

From 'The ABC of Cookery' 1945.

Make a list of wholesome and unwholesome foods.

Discuss your own diet. Do children today still get all the vitamins considered necessary in 1939?

How to avoid monotonous meals

A change of food does you good. That's why you so often enjoy a meal "out," or at a friend's. It's not that the cooking is better than your own. It's just that the dishes are made in a slightly different way.

Why not enjoy this change at home? Try adding a teaspoonful of Marmite to all your meat and vegetable dishes and see how the family sits up and takes notice. Marmite is a wonderful help to the busy housewife. It not only takes away the "sameness" from simple meals. It adds immensely to their nourishment and flavour.

There is a rich store of Vitamin B in Marmite which makes it a really protective health food. It stimulates the appetite, aids the digestion and builds up a powerful defence against illness. Stock your larder with a few jars of Marmite now.

A NEW POTATO DISH

You'll love baked stuffed potatoes done like this. You need potatoes, Marmite butter (made by mixing 3 parts margarine with one part Marmite), 1 egg, seasoning.
METHOD: Bake some large potatoes. Cut in halves, and scoop out inside. Mash with Marmite butter, pepper, salt, also a grate of nutmeg. Beat up the yolk of an egg and add to mashed potato. Whisk white of egg to a stiff froth and fold into mixture. Fill the jackets with this mixture and sprinkle with grated cheese. Thoroughly reheat in oven. Serve plain, or with tomato sauce.

MARMITE

(Registered Trade Mark)

DEFINITELY DOES YOU GOOD

Advertised Goods are Good Goods.   73

B. Here is a chart showing the heights of some boys and men in 1938. Measure as many boys and men of the same ages as you can and see how their heights compare.

BELOW: From 'Food and Planning' 1942.

Age.	London Elementary School, 1938.		Industrial Employees.		Secondary Schools.		Christ's Hospital, 1928–29.		Public School.		Students.		Australian Elementary School.		Los Angeles Elementary School.		Australian Public School.	
	In.	Cm.	In.	Cm.	In.	Cm.	In.	Cm.	In.	Cm.	In.	Cm.	In.	Cm.	In.	Cm.	In.	Cm.
5	43·0	109	—	—	—	—	—	—	—	—	—	—	—	—	46·0	117	—	—
6	45·2	114	—	—	—	—	—	—	—	—	—	—	—	—	48·2	122	—	—
7	47·4	120	—	—	—	—	—	—	—	—	—	—	—	—	50·4	128	—	—
8	49·5	125	—	—	—	—	—	—	—	—	—	—	—	—	52·5	133	—	—
9	51·5	131	—	—	—	—	51·8	131	—	—	—	—	—	—	54·4	138	—	—
10	53·5	135	—	—	—	—	53·4	135	—	—	—	—	—	—	56·3	140	—	—
11	55·3	140	—	—	—	—	55·3	140	—	—	—	—	53·6	136	58·3	149	56·6	143
12	57·0	144	—	—	—	—	56·9	144	—	—	—	—	55·6	141	60·6	153	58·3	149
13	58·7	149	—	—	57·3	145	58·9	149	62·7	159	—	—	57·0	144	63·3	161	62·0	157
14	—	—	61	154	60·2	153	61·1	154	63·6	161	—	—	59·0	150	65·5	166	61·8	156
15	—	—	63·2	160	64·9	164	64·0	162	66·6	169	—	—	61·4	155	67·3	171	65·4	166
16	—	—	65·3	166	66·0	167	66·0	167	69·2	176	—	—	—	—	68·9	174	67·7	171
17	—	—	66·3	168	66·8	167	67·7	174	69·6	178	68·3	173	—	—	68·0	175	68·9	176
18	—	—	66·1	168	67·0	170	68·9	175	70·6	179	68·6	174	—	—	—	—	68·0	175
19	—	—	67·1	170	68·3	174	69·4	176	70·7	179	68·8	175	—	—	—	—	—	—
20	—	—	67·2	170	—	—	—	—	—	—	68·9	175	—	—	—	—	—	—
21	—	—	67·3	171	—	—	—	—	—	—	68·6	175	—	—	—	—	—	—
22	—	—	67·2	170	—	—	—	—	—	—	68·5	174	—	—	—	—	—	—
23	—	—	67·4	171	—	—	—	—	—	—	68·3	173	—	—	—	—	—	—
24	—	—	67·3	171	—	—	—	—	—	—	68·4	173	—	—	—	—	—	—
25	—	—	67·4	171	—	—	—	—	—	—	68·3	173	—	—	—	—	—	—

Cooking and Energy Saving

A. Experiment with large biscuit-tins or the equivalent to see if you can build and use this method of cooking in camp-kettles and mess-tins. Please note that this experiment is dangerous and should only be attempted with appropriate safety measures.

PLATE 14.—COOKING IN CAMP KETTLES AND MESS TINS

PLAN.

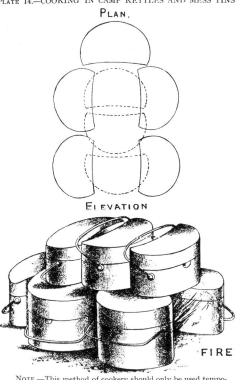

ELEVATION

FIRE

NOTE.—This method of cookery should only be used temporarily owing to the extravagant use of fuel. In standing camps the kettle trench (*see* plate 17, page 191) should be constructed.

PLATE 18
HOLE IN THE GROUND

Dig a hole about 1 foot deep and line the bottom and sides with bricks. The hole should be wide enough to take the cooking utensils in use, side by side, if necessary. Light a fire at the end of the hole nearer the prevailing wind. When hot enough to cook, remove the large embers on a metal plate, leaving the small embers on the bottom of the hole.

Place the foodstuffs in the hole and lay the metal plate with hot embers over the top of the hole.

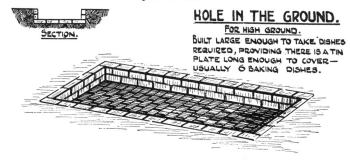

SECTION.

HOLE IN THE GROUND.
FOR HIGH GROUND.
BUILT LARGE ENOUGH TO TAKE DISHES REQUIRED, PROVIDING THERE IS A TIN PLATE LONG ENOUGH TO COVER — USUALLY 6 BAKING DISHES.

HOLE ABOVE THE GROUND

In low-lying country it is not always possible to dig a hole in the ground trench. The hole above the ground is constructed as above, except that it is built up and banked with earth.

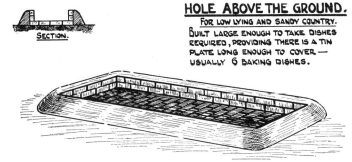

SECTION.

HOLE ABOVE THE GROUND.
FOR LOW LYING AND SANDY COUNTRY.
BUILT LARGE ENOUGH TO TAKE DISHES REQUIRED, PROVIDING THERE IS A TIN PLATE LONG ENOUGH TO COVER — USUALLY 6 BAKING DISHES.

B. Follow the instructions given to troops for making a cooking-fire on or in the ground.

Safety measures are also important when trying this experiment.

ABOVE, LEFT, & RIGHT: From the 'Manual of Military Cooking and Dietary' 1940.

C. Make a hay-box and experiment with this form of cooking. Make careful measurements and records.

These instructions are all from the War Office 'Manual of Military Cooking and Dietary' 1940.

PLATE 19.—HAY BOX

HAY BOX

APPENDIX VI
HAY BOX COOKERY

A specimen hay box has been provided at the School of Cookery, the detailed measurements as follows :—

Length	...	...	27 inches
Breadth	...	...	20 ,,
Height	...	...	22 ,,

It is constructed of $\frac{3}{8}$-inch tongued and grooved timber with corner battens of 2-inch by $\frac{1}{2}$-inch material.

It is fitted with :—

 i. A drop-on lid, packed with 2 inches of hay and covered with canvas.

 ii. A metal frame to fit the boiler for the purpose of keeping the walls of the hay packing in position.

 iii. A canvas frame to cover the hay to protect the food from hay seed and dust.

This box is sufficiently large to allow at least 3 inches of hay to be packed on the bottom and sides and a cushion of hay on top.

The experimental box made at the school of cookery weighs 140 lb. when packed with container filled ; therefore, 16 boxes would weigh 1 ton. Hay for packing weighs about 25 lb. and the hay and box without food container weigh 60 lb.

A tea chest packed with hay weighs 40 lb., and when packed with food 120 lb. 18 of these can be carried on a light six-wheeler, the load being approximately 1 ton.

The hay used must be perfectly dry, and should be pressed firmly into the bottom of the box to a depth of 3 inches. Then place the metal frame and boiler into the centre of the box and press hay all round it level with the top of the boiler. Finally remove the boiler, leaving the metal frame in the mould. Place the prepared food in the boiler and bring to the boil on an ordinary fire. After it has boiled the necessary time, see that the lid is tightly secured and without delay place the boiler into the mould whilst the contents are still on the boil. Now fill in the top with a cushion made by placing hay in a sack and press tightly. Put on the lid, which should fit closely.

Special points which must be strictly observed are :—

 i. Hay must be pressed tightly all over. If the hay is loose in any part of the box the heat can escape and the temperature of the food will quickly fall.

 ii. If the boiler is taken out of the box for any reason before the food is required, it must always be brought to boiling-point before being returned to the box.

 iii. All foods must be placed in the box at boiling-point, 212° Fahr.

 iv. When the temperature drops to 130° Fahr. it will fall quickly, and such food as porridge or stewed meat with vegetables will begin to ferment. Only food at a temperature of 140° Fahr. or over can be described as a hot meal.

 v. The hay box will not cook any foodstuff which requires top heat or rapid boiling all the time ; therefore it will not roast or fry, and will not boil flour puddings or cabbage. Roast and fried meat and boiled puddings must be completely cooked before being placed in the box. If left in the box for a long time, roast meat will become stringy and flavourless, and boiled puddings will become soggy.

Provided the food is boiling when placed in the hay box, and the box properly packed, it will remain hot for 20 hours. In summer time, when the temperature of the atmosphere is high, the food will remain hot for a longer period. The containers must always be full when placed in the hay box.

Certain food will continue to cook if put in the hay box at boiling-point. It will not cook pastry, which requires the top heat of an oven, or pudding, which requires the contents of a cooking vessel to be kept at boiling-point. It will not cook cabbage or certain vegetables which should boil rapidly. There is a great saving of fuel, and the hay box should invariably be used when cooking for small units, detachments, guards, picquets, etc.

The following Timetable for hay-box cookery has been compiled from experience gained in the treating of various foodstuffs in an ordinary service camp kettle.

Article	Men	Hours Soaking	Boiling on a fire	Minimum time in box
IRISH STEW AND DUMPLINGS.	15	—	Bring to boil and boil for 10 minutes. Add dumplings and boil another 8 minutes.	Hours 3
STEWED STEAK...	30	—	20 mins. after frying	2
BOILED HAM OR BACON	10	12	30 minutes	6
MEAT PUDDINGS	20	—	As for Irish stew ...	3
SEA PIE	15	—	Do.	3
BOILED BEEF AND CARROTS	15	—	30 minutes	3
POTATOES... ...	30	—	5 minutes	1½
GREEN PEAS ...	30	—	Bring to boil only ...	1
BLUE PEAS ...	20	12	30 minutes	3
HARICOT BEANS	20	12	30 minutes	3
BUTTER BEANS...	20	12	30 minutes	3
STEWED PRUNES	30	12	5 minutes	1½
STEWED FIGS ...	30	12	5 minutes	1½
MIXED FRUIT ...	20	12	Bring to boil only ...	1½

The following is a timetable for hay-box cookery, using 6-gallon insulated containers.

6-GALLON INSULATED CONTAINERS

Article	Men	Soaking Hours	Boiling on a fire	Minimum time in box
IRISH STEW AND DUMPLINGS	30	—	Bring to boil for 10 minutes. Add dumplings and boil another 8 minutes.	Hours 3
BOILED HAM OR BACON.	50	12	30 minutes	6
STEWED STEAKS	75	—	20 mins. after frying	2
MEAT PUDDINGS	50	—	As for Irish stew ...	3
SEA PIE	36	—	As for Irish stew ...	3
BOILED BEEF AND CARROTS.	36	—	30 minutes	3
POTATOES... ...	60	—	5 minutes	1
GREEN PEAS ...	100	—	Bring to boil only ...	1
BLUE PEAS ...	100	12	30 minutes	3
HARICOT BEANS	100	12	30 minutes	3
BUTTER BEANS...	100	12	30 minutes	3
STEWED PRUNES	75	12	5 minutes	1½
STEWED FIGS ...	75	12	5 minutes	1½
MIXED FRUIT ...	75	12	Bring to boil only ...	1½

Points to Notice

 i. Keep the hay as dry as possible.

 The soup or tea must always be poured into the prepared tin boiling hot.

 iii. The tin must be scalded out each time it is used. This can be done without removing it from the pack.

 iv. The same pack and hay will last for weeks.

 v. If hay should get wet it must be dried and repacked before being used again.

Advertising

Although commercial advertising was actually restricted during the war because of lack of space in magazines and scarcity of paper for printing - not to mention a scarcity of goods as shown in these illustrations - Government advertisements are one of our richest sources of evidence. The Government was able to capitalise on people's good will.

"The methods of war may be horrible to the verge of idiocy. But war has this redeeming sanity, that its purpose is clear and the methods that it uses are logically directed towards the achievement of that purpose. It is the feeling of common and intelligible purpose, far more than any heroics, that reconciles people to war. The chaos of production for private and conflicting interests goes. The ploughman in the fields, the sailor and fisherman are not just getting something to be sold, or thrown away if the price offered is too low; they are supplying the needs of the people." 'Food and Planning' J.R. Marrack 1942

A. Look at the advertisements illustrated in this book and find modern advertisements for the same products/brand-names. Can you find less evidence of "private and conflicting interests" in the war-time advertisements?

You can still get as many cups of good coffee from each bottle of 'Camp' as you used to enjoy before the war. But there are not so many bottles of 'Camp' available today. Like other good things, supplies of 'Camp' are still limited, but you should get your share if you ask for it by name.

FAMOUS FOR STRENGTH AND FLAVOUR

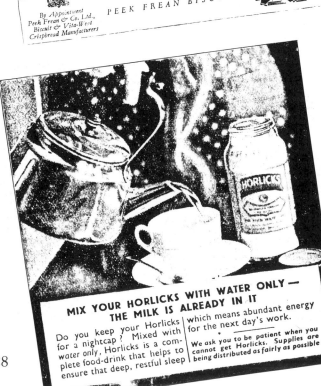

MIX YOUR HORLICKS WITH WATER ONLY — THE MILK IS ALREADY IN IT

Do you keep your Horlicks for a nightcap? Mixed with water only, Horlicks is a complete food-drink that helps to ensure that deep, restful sleep | which means abundant energy for the next day's work.

We ask you to be patient when you cannot get Horlicks. Supplies are being distributed as fairly as possible

Until then . . . When toffee apples are two-a-penny and little Tommy's only danger is a sisterly smack for being greedy, the whole world will be at peace to enjoy the fruits of the earth. Until then, if we follow the advice of those who are in charge of supplies the foods and fruits in Britain will last longer and go further. If by eating more potatoes we can save more bread then let's all feel delighted to do so. And if we don't get any fatter we *are* becoming a healthier nation.

FORD MOTOR COMPANY LIMITED, DAGENHAM, ESSEX   LONDON SHOWROOMS : 88, REGENT STREET, W.1

B. Compare the language, style of drawing or photos, the clothes the people are wearing and the audience the advertisements seem to be aimed at with modern advertisements. The advertisement has become a source of evidence for history - like a Roman wall painting or a medieval manuscript - in addition to the message it contains.

C. Find a Government advertisement issued today and compare it with the ones in this book. Is it as straightforward as the war-time advertisements? If not, why not?

The Pick of the Crop

Batchelor's Peas

IT'S THE FLAVOUR THAT'S IN FAVOUR

A little **BOVRIL** *puts beef into it*

In bottles—1oz. 10d · 2 oz. 1/6d · 4 oz.

Glorious **CURLS** and **WAVES** *Overnight*

For hair that always looks lovely use LORELOX. Combs hair to curl and stay curled. Harmless and not sticky.

It isn't Luck... it's **LORELOX** 2/7½ PER BOTTLE TAX PAID

Will soon be easier to obtain from all Chemists

...is best food value for points and pence **Weetabix**

MORE than a Breakfast Food

Prices: 8d. Large size 1/2. Sold everywhere. Supplies limited.
WEETABIX LTD., BURTON LATIMER, NORTHANTS

Domestic Ease begins with these....

"Tala" KITCHENWARE for Beauty and Efficiency

BUILD UP YOUR KITCHEN EQUIPMENT FROM "TALA" KITCHENWARE AS IT COMES BACK TO THE SHOPS. MOST "ESSENTIALS" AND SOME "DESIRABLES" ARE ON THE MARKET—BUT NOT ALWAYS PLENTIFUL.

TAYLOR, LAW & CO. LTD., STOURBRIDGE & BIRMINGHAM

OVERALL DEPARTMENT

" Ah, my dear, I see you use Persil ! "

No MISTAKING Persil whiteness ! And you get the same brilliant results with Persil for the rest of the wash. Those gentle but marvellously cleansing Persil suds make coloureds sparkle, fine silks and rayons beautifully lustrous, woollens soft and springy. There's nothing to equal Persil *for the whole wash.*

PERSIL WASHES WHITER

Analysing the Evidence

> "The past is a foreign country: they do things differently there."
> 'The Go-Between' L.P. Hartley 1953

This book is full of information which can be used for historical analysis.

A. Identity Documents. Compare those used in the war with those we have today: Driving licences, passports, National Insurance cards, Bank cards. Discuss the major change implied by the invention of plastic credit cards. In most European countries they still have Identity Cards.

Martello Tower, near Bawdsey in Suffolk. These towers were part of a defence for the south east and East Anglian coasts built because of the threat of invasion by Napoleon in the early nineteenth century. This one, like many others, was pressed into service again during the war and had a gun emplacement built onto its roof.

	Price in 1945	Price in Feb 1990
	s. d.	
Bread	4½ per 2lb loaf	64p (large unsliced white loaf)
Eggs	2 0 per dozen (large)	1.20p per dozen (large)
Sugar	4 per lb	25p per lb
Milk	4½ per pint	30p per pint
Tea	8½ per quarter lb	49p per quarter

B. Pounds, shillings and pence can be discussed and pupils can bring in pre-decimal coinage for examination.

C. Some of the material used in the book was collected from relatives and friends. Pupils could ask their own families for objects and documents from this period so that they can have actual evidence.

D.
Looking for the past in the landscape.

Our surroundings, in both town and country, still contain evidence of the Second World War. Pillboxes, strongly built of concrete and reinforced with iron, are a formidable obstruction to farmers today. Air-raid shelters constructed at the bottom of gardens often remain part of the garden landscape.

The illustrations here show how much has survived. The buildings and defences of the war are preserved as ancient monuments today and, like Roman forts and medieval town walls, are protected by legislation.

ABOVE & BELOW: Pevensey Fort, East Sussex was originally a Roman fort built to protect the coast of Britain in the middle of the fourth century AD. Its wall was reused when the site was chosen as a castle after the Norman invasion. In May 1940 it became an observation and command post and had pillboxes cleverly built into its walls. It was in continuous use by the Home Guard and regular troops, including Canadian and American soldiers, until 1944.

LEFT: Anti-tank ditches were cut to standard dimensions across vulnerable routes. This one, now filled in and showing as a soil mark in Bradfield in Essex, was originally a nineteenth century railway cutting (never completed) which had also been dug out as a defence during the First World War.

P.F. Jenner

'Dragon's Teeth', as they were called by the popular press, were part of the anti-tank defences hurriedly constructed in 1940. These, at Waverley Abbey in Surrey, were photographed during a school project.

Mike Corbishley

General Sir Edmund Ironside, Commander-in-Chief Home Forces, initiated the building of thousands of pillboxes in June 1940 to protect the coast of Britain and some major centres. Pillboxes guarded lines of communication such as roads, canals and railway lines as well as providing the defences along possible invasion beaches. This pillbox is in north east Essex.

Don Rumble

Mike Corbishley

In the back garden of a semi-detached in south London stands an air raid shelter. Partly disguised, it has been used as a garden shed since the war.

Mike Corbishley

Beacon Hill, Harwich, Essex was fortified under Henry VIII. Gun batteries were constructed there in the nineteenth century and updated during the First World War. This photograph shows a look-out tower from the Second World War. Notice the attempt at camouflage by painting window frames with curtains on the walls!

The housing crisis caused by bombing made the government turn to 'temporary' housing. There are still a few pre-fabs left but these, built in 1947 at Little Oakley in Essex, were demolished in 1975 to make way for a new housing estate.

The Western Heights at Dover have seen a number of massive fortifications dating from the pre-Roman iron age. The great medieval castle was strengthened and modernized during the wars with France in the late eighteenth and early nineteenth centuries.

The underground casements built then were re-used during the First World War. In the Second World War these tunnels, nearly 200 feet below ground, became the naval headquarters of Vice-Admiral Bertram Ramsey. It was from here that Vice-Admiral Ramsey directed naval and civilian ships to evacuate the troops from Dunkirk in 1940.

In 1942 these underground works were extended to include a hospital with a dressing station, an operating theatre, dormitories and a kitchen.

BELOW: Dover Castle from the air.

Try Your Own Recipes

A. Try making some of the recipes listed, in school.

B. Make 'Mock Marzipan', 'Cake or Pudding' or 'Pink Layer Party Cake' and ask others to taste and guess the ingredients used.

C. Make a survey of local supermarkets and shops to see whether most of the ingredients used in the recipes are still there today.

List foods which were scarce during rationing: e.g. bananas, lemons, oranges.

List foods which we buy today which were not imported to Britain at all then: e.g. Tortilla chips, sweet potatoes, stuffed vine-leaves.

D. Try spending a complete week on a ration book diet. Record your feelings about it and your weight difference. Did you feel healthier? Here is one week's ration for one adult:

Milk	3 pints
Sugar	225gm (8oz)
Butter	50gm (2oz)
Margarine	100gm (4oz)
Cooking fat	85gm (3oz)
Cheese	85gm (3oz)
Bacon	100gm (4oz)
Meat	to the value of 1s 2d (2d had to be spent on corned beef)

(holders of Child's Ration Book RB2 got one half of these amounts of meat)

Eggs	1 (if available) and 1 packet of dried eggs per month
Sweets	60gm (2.1oz)
Jam	50gm (2oz)
Tea	50gm (2oz)

The following were NOT rationed during the war:

Sausages (but hard to obtain)
Bread
Potatoes
Vegetables

Mike Corbishley

Fiction

Read a work of fiction in which the action occurs during the war. See Bibliography for a selected list.

Dried eggs and Spam are still available in supermarkets today.

Bibliography

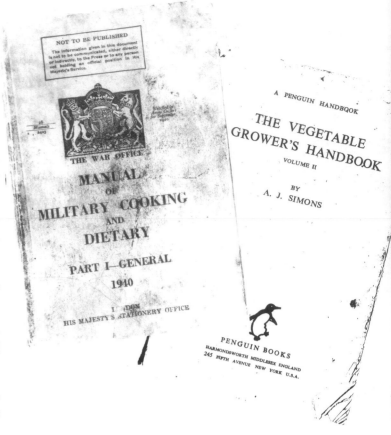

Contemporary Books and Documents

'The ABC of Cookery'. HMSO 1945.

Food Education Memoranda from the Board of Education. 'Salads and Vegetables', 'Good Fare in War Time', 'Food from Overseas'. His Majesty's Stationery Office 1941.

'Good Eating: Suggestions for Wartime Dishes' published by Hutchinson from 'reader tested recipes' in the Daily Telegraph. Undated.

'Good Fare' compiled by the Daily Telegraph Home Cook. Hutchinson. Undated.

Good Housekeeping Bulletins, for example, 'No.10 Thrifty Wartime Meals', 'No.11 Recipes and Menus that Save Fuel' and 'No.14 Fruit Bottling in Wartime'. Undated.

Growmore Bulletins from the Ministry of Agriculture and Fisheries. For example 'Food from the Garden' and 'Preserves from the Garden'. HMSO 1940.

'The Kitchen Front' Nicholson and Watson 1942. 122 recipes selected from the BBC programme of the same name.

'Manual of Military Cooking and Dietary Part 1 - General' issued by the War Office. HMSO 1940.

Marrack, J R, 'Food and Planning' Victor Gollancz 1942. Detailed research into diet and nutrition from the nineteenth century to 1942.

'100 Recipes for Unrationed Meat Dishes' published by Good Housekeeping. Undated.

Plimmer, Violet G, 'Food Values in Wartime' Longmans & Green 1941. More popular and readable version of Marrack's Food and Planning'.

'Stork Margarine Cookery Notes' for example, 'New Ways with Winter Vegetables' No.81 January 1947.

'War Time Cookery Book' published by the Daily Express in November 1939.

'Wartime "Good Housekeeping" Cookery Book' compiled by the Good Housekeeping Institute. Penguin 1942.

Social History/Recipe Books

Braithwaite, Brian & Walsh, Noelle & Davies, Glyn (compilers), 'The Home Front: The Best of Good Housekeeping 1939-1945' Ebury Press 1987. ISBN O-85223-607-7. Collected articles, advertisements and recipes from Good Housekeeping.

Briggs, Susan, 'Keep Smiling Through: The Home Front 1939-45' 1975 Weidenfeld and Nicolson 1975. ISBN 0-297-76989-8. A good introduction to the period with many illustrations.

Minns, Raynes, 'Bombers and Mash: The Domestic Front 1939-45' Virago 1980. ISBN 0-86068-041-X. Puts the propaganda story straight on the involvement of women in the war at home. Contains many recipes.

Patten, Maguerite, 'We'll Eat Again' Hamlyn 1985. ISBN 0-600-32524-5. Published in association with the Imperial War Museum it is mainly recipes and food facts.

Waller, Jane & Vaughan-Rees, Michael, 'Women in Wartime: The role of Women's Magazines 1939-1945' Macdonald 1987. ISBN 0-356-12887-3. A good introduction to this valuable source of evidence.

English Heritage has published a series of books on Food and Cooking in Britain:

Renfrew, J 'Food and Cooking in Prehistoric Britain' 1985. ISBN 1-85074-079-8.

Renfrew, J 'Food and Cooking in Roman Britain' 1985. ISBN 1-85074-080-1.

Black, M 'Food and Cooking in Medieval Britain' 1985. ISBN 1-85074-081-X.

Brears, P 'Food and Cooking in 16th Century Britain' 1985. ISBN 1-85074082-8.

Brears, P 'Food and Cooking in 17th Century Britain' 1985. ISBN 1-850-74-083-6

Stead, J 'Food and Cooking in 18th Century Britain' 1985. ISBN 1-85074-084-4

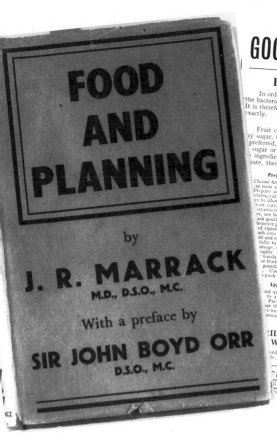

Black, M 'Food and Cooking in 19th Century Britain' 1985. ISBN 1-85074-085-2

Books for classwork
Allen, Eleanor, 'Wartime Children 1939-1945' A & C Black 1975. ISBN 0-7136-1503-6. Good textbook for middle school pupils.

Chrisp, Peter with Coate, Leslie, 'Children in Wartime: 1939-1945' Tressel Publications 1989. ISBN 0 907586 72 4. Collection of children's writing. Pupil's study notes available which may be copied. ISBN 0-907586-73-2.

Holley, Erica, 'Food' Dryad Press 1985. ISBN 0-8521-9640-7. One of the Timeline series for 14-17 year olds which explores the historical evidence for food in Britain from prehistory to the twentieth century.

'The Home Front: Documents relating to life in Britain, 1939-1945' Imperial War Museum 1987. ISBN 0-901627-39-9. Pack of facsimile documents (such as ration book, poster) for school project work.

Kelsall, Freda. 'How we used to live 1900-1945' Macdonald 1976. ISBN 0-356-05484-5. Published as background reading for Yorkshire Television's series of the same name.

Pike, Alastair & Anne, 'The Home Front in Britain 1939-45' Tressell Publications 1985. ISBN 0-907586-16-3. Oral and contemporary accounts collected by two history teachers.

'Rationing in Great Britain during the Second World War' Information Sheet No 20 available from the Imperial War Museum. A detailed account of foods rationed and de-rationed giving precise dates and weights of food.

Reynoldson, Fiona, 'War at Home' Heinemann 1980, ISBN 0-435-31880-2. Interesting text with activities (such as crosswords) and project work for middle school pupils.

Novels quoted in text
Bowen, Elizabeth, 'The Heat of the Day' Jonathan Cape 1949.

Blishen Edmund, 'A Cack-handed War' Thames and Hudson 1972. ISBN 0-500-01082-X

Hartley, L P, 'The Go-Between' Hamish Hamilton 1953. Available in Penguin. ISBN 0-241-90208-8

Powell, Anthony, 'A Dance to the Music of Time 8: The Soldier's Art' Collins 1966. Available as a Fontana Paperback. ISBN 0-00-654049-X.

Macauley, Rose, 'The World my Wilderness' Collins 1950. Available from Virago Press. ISBN 0-002-21927-1.

Thirkell, Angela, 'Growing Up'. Book Club 1945.

Novels for children.

Bawden. Nina, 'Carrie's War' Heinemann 1973. ISBN 0-435-12202-9. Story of an evacuated brother and sister. Age 11+.

Grant, Gwen, 'Private, Keep Out' Collins 1986. ISBN 0-006-716520-0. Midlands family just after the war. Age 10+.

Kerr, Judith, 'The Other Way Round' Collins 1986. ISBN 0-006-71234-7. German refugee family in wartime London. Age 11-14.

Streatfeild, Noel, 'When the Siren Wailed' Collins 1986. ISBN 0-00671238-X. Evacuees from east London. Age 9-11.

Trease, Geoffrey, 'Tomorrow is a Stranger' Pan 1989. ISBN 0-330-30903-X. Set in Guernsey in 1940. Age 9-12.

Westall, Robert, 'The Machine Gunners' Macmillan 1977. ISBN 0-333-27868-2. Boys rescue a machine gun from a crashed German aeroplane. Age 11+.

Collected poems
Harvey, Ann, 'In Time of War' Blackie 1987. ISBN 0-216-92324-7. Poems about the two world wars published in association with the Imperial War Museum.

Finding out more
Contemporary documents and archives may be available in your County Record Office or in the reference collection in the local library. Try your local newspaper for photocopies or microfilms.

Study material on the Second World War has been published by several Local Education Authorities or Teachers' Centres, often in association with the County Record Office.

Collections of old photos are often published as booklets by library services or history societies.

Local or county museums usually have some collections relating to the last war. Ask about handling them in the museum or the availability of loan collections for schools.

The Imperial War Museum has the largest collection of objects and documents and may be contacted at Lambeth Road, London SE1 6HZ. Tel: 01-735 8922.

Pillboxes have been studied in depth recently. A detailed account is published by Wills, Henry, 'Pillboxes' Leo Cooper in association with Secker and Warburg 1985. ISBN 0-436-57360-1.

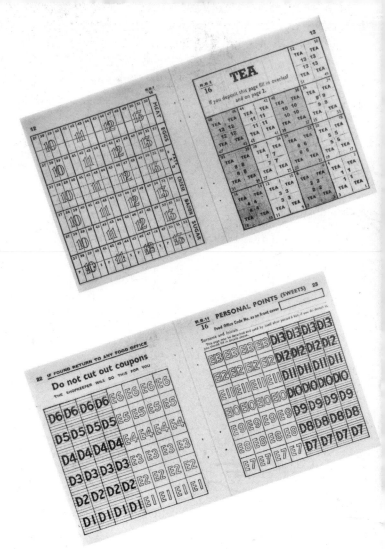

Acknowledgements

The author and English Heritage gratefully acknowledge the help given by Jenny Pile, Psyche Corbishley, Elizabeth Rumble, Margaret Booker, Barbara Bache, Mary Chrystal and Peggy Lord. Permission to reproduce extracts from published work has kindly been given by:

Collins/Virago Press (for 'The World My Wilderness'), Thames and Hudson (for 'A Cack-handed War'), Jonathan Cape (for 'The Heat of the Day'), Collins (for 'A Dance to the Music of Time'), Batsford (for 'Food'), Heinemann (for 'War at Home').

The following suppliers have kindly allowed us to reproduce advertisements and photographs:

Parish and Fenn (for Spam), Crookes Healthcare (for Ostermilk), Van den Berghs (for Stork), HP Heinz, Beecham Bovril Brands (for Bovril and Marmite), Wanda (for Ovaltine), Good Housekeeping, Punch (for cartoon on page 12), Prestige, Weetabix, Brooke Bond Foods (for Batchelor's Peas), Jacob's Bakery (for Peek Frean), and the Ford Motor Company. Her Majesty's Stationery Office and The Ministry of Agriculture, Fisheries and Food gave permission to reproduce Crown Copyright government advertisements and leaflets.

We have made every effort to find the owners of the copyright of material in this book and apologise to any we have not located.

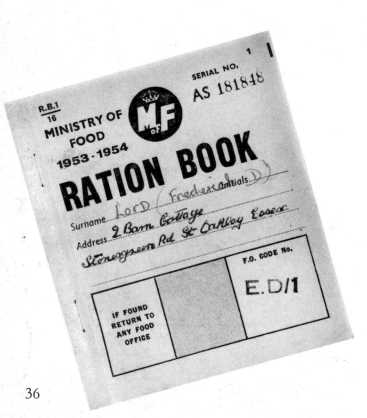

RIGHT: Mrs Witham, mother of sixteen, works out her ration quota for the family.
BACK COVER: Mrs Ann Smith aged 62 of Wandsworth, London tosses pieces of her ration books into the air at the end of rationing 5 July 1954. Hulton Picture Library